MERLANTIS

First Edition: August 2017

Editor: Charlotte C. Breslin, www.SkeletonKeyEditing.com
Book Designer: K.R. Conway, CapeCodScribe.com
Illustrator: Aljon Inertia, aljoncomahig@gmail.com

Library of Congress Cataloging-in-Publication Data
Mermaid, Music
Merlantis/ by Music Mermaid – First Edition.
        Pages: 38
    Summary: Mermaid princess Sharon of Merlantis loves to sing and make friends. When she is given a chance to go to the land to meet people with her merdog, Nemo, she finds new friends and returns to her ocean home with new songs to sing to the merpeople of Merlantis.

Music Mermaid
Dedham, MA
www.MusicMermaid.com

ISBN: 978-0-692-91780-0

Published in the United States of America

Music for Merlantis

This book contains lyrics to dance songs which can be listened to while you read along. The songs can be found for free at www.MusicMermaid.com and on Music Mermaid's Soundcloud and YouTube channels.

The songs are also available on CDBABY, iTunes, Googleplay, and Amazon Music. Simply search for the album name "Merlantis" or artist name, "Music Mermaid."

"My dream has always been to make a positive difference in the lives of others. We need a world full of love and kindness."

Arielle & Ripleigh!

You are s'awesome ♡ ✿

www.MusicMermaid.com

♡MM & NLS

Once upon a time there was a mermaid princess named Sharon who lived in Merlantis with her parents and brother and sister.

Her favorite color was red and she loved to sing. Happy and curious, she would meet her many friends as she swam in the ocean all day long.

Sharon had a gift for making music.

Whenever she was excited about something, she would come up with a dance song.

Sharon loved to dance, and making people dance made her very happy.

When Sharon was 11 years old, her Mer-Godmother gave her the best gift ever: a merdog named Nemo Lucky Sharky.

When Nemo and Sharon met, they hugged each other and instantly became best friends.

Sharon took Nemo everywhere she went, for she loved Nemo more than anything in the world.

And Nemo loved Sharon, for he was loyal and friendly and would always stay by Sharon's side.

Nemo loved to hear
Sharon sing, and sometimes
he would sing along.
His favorite song was about a
magical place called Manlantis.

Sharon knew about Manlantis
from the stories told by other
mermaids who could only go there
for 1 day on their 19th birthday with
the help of their Mer-Godmothers.

It was a beautiful place, with a
sun and moon. It was a place where
everyone had legs and they danced
and laughed and loved life.

Oh, how Sharon longed to
go to Manlantis. But she
knew she would have
to wait, just as the other
mermaids had, until her
19th birthday.

Manlantis

There's a place I long to see
Far away above the sea
Somewhere new that's not so blue
Fun and wild and fancy free!

Manlantis Manlantis
where you see the moon
Manlantis Manlantis
hope we'll be there soon

Verse 2
When we're there you'll feel the sun!
We can play and we can run!
All around our life can be
Bright and light so happy!

Chorus/Refrain
Manlantis Manlantis,
where you see the moon
Manlantis Manlantis,
hope we'll be there soon

Years passed, and on Sharon's 18th birthday, her father, King Edmond, asked her what she wanted most. So Sharon told her father that she and Nemo would like to visit Manlantis now, and not wait until her 19th birthday.

Her brother Sami was very protective of Sharon and became concerned when she asked to go to Manlantis, but the king remembered how much he enjoyed going when he was young.

And so, the king granted Sharon permission to go. She was told to follow the rules of her Mer-Godmother.

Mer-Godmothers have the ability to travel between Manlantis and Merlantis.

The next morning, Sharon's Mer-Godmother, Carol, appeared to wish Sharon a happy birthday.

She granted Sharon and Nemo legs and the ability to breathe and talk on Manlantis. "You and Nemo may visit Manlantis for only 1 day," she told them.

Carol also told Sharon that her family loved her very much and for her to be safe.

"Have fun!" she said, and granted Sharon's wish.

When Sharon and Nemo arrived on the shore of Manlantis, it was just as beautiful as she dreamed it would be.

After walking many miles on Manlantis, Sharon and Nemo spotted a lovely garden ahead. In the garden, Sharon began to sing and dance as Nemo skipped to the beat and chased after a lady bug.

Moments later, a red-haired boy and his dog, who were passing by, joined in the dancing. He loved Sharon's song and told her that ladybugs were lucky, and if they fly away after you make a wish and blow on them, the wish will come true.

Sharon had never met anyone with red hair, and because she loved the color red so much, she called the boy Red. Nemo also made friends with Red's dog, Boston.

Red invited Sharon and Nemo to his house for a lunch party.

LUCKY LADYBUG

Verse 1
Flashback to my childhood
I saw you sitting there on a flower
Ooh, I knew it you were gonna bring me the power, oh!

Chorus / Refrain
Lucky Lucky ladybug, lucky!
Lucky Lucky ladybug, lucky!

Verse 2
Yah, I can feel it
My luck is looking very good today
No fear in the New Year
Things are gonna go my way!

Lucky Lucky ladybug, lucky!
Lucky Lucky ladybug, lucky!

Verse 3
Feel it inside you
One love got the power
No hate and darkness
Shine bright like a flower, Yah!

Lucky Lucky ladybug, lucky!
Lucky Lucky ladybug, lucky!

When Sharon and Nemo
arrived at Red's house,
Red's mother, Ju Lee,
was so happy to see them.

Sharon could not believe her eyes
when she saw Ju Lee's garden, for
she had never seen anything so
beautiful.

The garden was filled with delicate
flowers in many colors. There were
birds and a pond with lily pads and
the cutest frogs she had ever seen.

Sharon met Red's friends Bruno,
Anoki, and Melody.

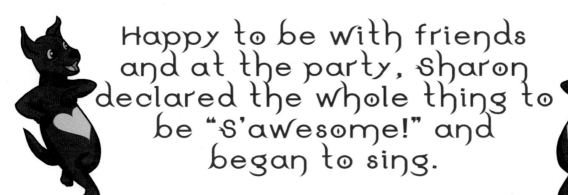

Happy to be with friends
and at the party, Sharon
declared the whole thing to
be "S'awesome!" and
began to sing.

Sharon and Nemo stayed
at Red's house and
had a great night's sleep.
What a fun day they had.

Nemo reminded Sharon that they
had to leave. Sharon was very sad,
but she knew she could not break her
promise to her Mer-Godmother.

Red did not want them to leave and
Sharon began to cry. They hugged
each other very tightly, but suddenly
Sharon and Nemo disappeared. Her
journey to Manlantis was over and it
was time to return to Merlantis.

Red and his mother were
shocked and saddened that
the girl they had come
to love couldn't stay, but
they knew Sharon had a
family beneath the waves
waiting for her.

When Sharon and Nemo returned to Merlantis, all the merfolk and sea animals were so happy to see them.

Sharon's brother, Sami, who swam as fast as he could to greet them, cried, "You must never leave again!" and hugged her.

King Edmond and Queen Nancy had arranged a party with a stage so Sharon could sing some of the Kingdom's favorite songs, and so Sharon began to sing. Sharon started her performance with her new songs, "S'awesome" and "Lucky Ladybug."

Everyone began to dance.

S'awesome

Verse 1
Everything about this place
Puts a smile on my face
When I look around I see
Everything is so happy!

Chorus / Refrain
S'awesome S'awesome
S'awesome S'awesome!
S'awesome S'awesome S'awesome
S'awesome S'awesome! (Repeat)

Verse 2
Look on up into the sky
What is that A dragon fly?!
Look around and you will see
Love and light; I feel so free!

Chorus / Refrain
S'awesome S'awesome
S'awesome S'awesome!
S'awesome S'awesome S'awesome
S'awesome S'awesome! (Repeat)

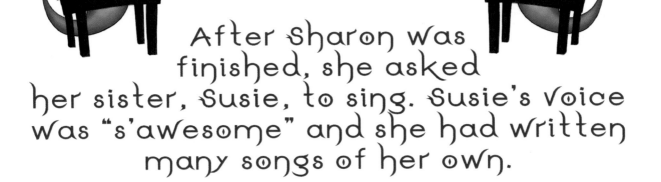

After Sharon was finished, she asked her sister, Susie, to sing. Susie's voice was "s'awesome" and she had written many songs of her own.

While Sharon was dancing with Nemo, a handsome merman started to dance with them.

Sharon recognized him. He was Fin, an old friend who had moved away years ago to a different kingdom.

Fin told Sharon that he had missed her all these years and couldn't wait to spend time with her again.

Fin and Sharon spent
every day together
and soon they decided
they wanted to marry.

So Fin met with King Edmond and
asked for Sharon's hand in marriage.
King Edmond said he would prefer
Sharon marry a prince, for she was a
princess. Sharon's mother,
Nancy, disagreed.

"I know Fin's family," she said.
"They've just moved back to the
Kingdom. Fin's mother is a doctor who
helps many merfolk. Fin is a hard
worker and kind. Although he is not
a prince, he loves Sharon.
Let Sharon decide."

So Edmond granted Fin
permission to marry
Sharon.

The next day, Fin asked Sharon to officially marry him.

He told her that he would always love her and protect her, and provide for her and Nemo forever.

Sami and Susie were so happy that they would soon have a new merbrother! Sharon was excited and knew that no matter how much fun she had once had on Manlantis, she could never leave Merlantis, because her merfamily was the most important thing to her.

The king and queen announced to the kingdom the plans for the royal wedding, and everyone was happy.

 Sharon, Fin, Nemo, and all the merfolk of Merlantis lived happily ever after . . .

A Special Thank You from Music Mermaid!

To my father Edmond, mother Nancy, brother Sami and sister Susie, and especially my dog, Nemo Lucky Sharky! Thank you for all your love and support.

To my awesome cousin, Sami's daughter Christina, who suggested I write a children's book after hearing my dance songs in Lebanon during the summer of 2015. Lebanon is where my book was written. It is a beautiful country, and if you are ever given a chance, please do go and visit!

To my Great Uncle Tony, who gave my family the joy of living by the beautiful south shore beaches of Massachusetts. And to my Godfather Antoun, who was so kind. Memory Eternal!

To my fellow teachers and good friends Annie and Brian. Brian did the initial edits of Merlantis for me! And to my friends Scott, Orman, Aya, Joanne and Katie and Bruno, who were the first to donate to my Go Fund Me. Thanks for believing in me!

To my awesome illustrator, Aljon Inertia, whose art fills these pages. And to Hans Christian Anderson, who wrote the original story of The Little Mermaid in 1836, and to Disney, for reviving the story for a whole new generation.

To Peter Reynolds, who encouraged me and mentored me when I told him I wanted to write a children's book. If you haven't read his books yet you need to check them out: http://www.peterhreynolds.com

Lastly, a huge thank you to author K.R. Conway for helping me format Merlantis. She and her books can be found at www.CapeCodScribe.com and on Twitter @sharkprose.

Music Mermaid's Story

Music Mermaid is a Lebanese-American woman and was born in Roslindale, Massachusetts.
She lived in Kuwait for 8 years of her childhood.
Today she teaches elementary school music.

Her connection with the ocean and love for mermaids started when she was a child at her great uncle Tony's beach house in Massachusetts. MM wrote this book in honor of this man, who loved beautiful things and his family. In Kuwait, MM's family belonged to a sports club on the beach. Kuwait was very hot, so every summer her family would return to uncle Tony's beach house.

MM decided to be a Music Educator because her mother thought she would be really good at it. MM received her Bachelor's degree in Music Education from University of Massachusetts Boston. She also has a Masters of Music Education from Gordon College, and a Communications and Film Bachelor's degree from UMASS Amherst.

"Nothing compares to the feeling of happiness I get from seeing my students become confident in their singing, dancing, music literacy, acting and speaking skills. Please support the Arts in public schools." - MM

www.MusicMermaid.com

Made in the USA
Middletown, DE
25 October 2020